Rules for Reaching Consensus

Rules for Reaching Consensus

A Modern Approach to Decision Making

Steven Saint and James R. Lawson

Amsterdam • Johannesburg • Oxford
San Diego • Sydney • Toronto

Editor: JoAnn Padgett
Associate Editor: Heidi Erika Callinan
Production Editor: Katharine Pechtimaldjian
Page Compositor: Judy Whalen
Cover: John Odam Design Associates

Library of Congress Cataloging-in-Publication Data
Lawson, James (James R.)
    Rules for reaching consensus: a modern approach to the age-old
process of making decisions / James Lawson and Steven Saint.
        p.   cm.
    Includes index.
    ISBN: 0-89384-256-7 (pbk.)
    1. Work groups.   2. Decision-making, Group.   3. Consensus
(Social sciences)   I. Saint, Steven.   II. Title.
HD66.L38   1994
658.4'036—dc20   94-4486
                                                            CIP

Printed in the United States of America.

Printing 1 2 3 4 5 6 7 8 9 10

Dedication

To C.T. Butler and Food Not Bombs—
thanks for turning on the light.

Contents

Introduction

Organizations today must be responsive to rapidly changing events. Trends such as downsizing, decentralizing, outsourcing of jobs and work, creating teams, the increasing use of advanced technologies, a shifting emphasis from manufacturing to knowledge workers, and implementing total quality management practices all contribute to the breakdown of the hierarchical organization with its command-and-control style of management.

Organizations of the twenty-first century are evolving into dynamic systems comprised of networked teams of educated knowledge workers. Brain power versus capital and manual labor drive business and industry. Authority is shifting from traditional seats of power to those with the knowledge and the ability to apply that knowledge.

Solo decision making is giving way to collective decision making. The manager's role is shifting from making decisions to empowering others to make decisions. Those most knowledgeable and closest to the problem are becoming key to the decision-making process.

Due to this shift, manager's new role is to facilitate collective decision making among diverse individuals and teams. The purpose of this book is to help managers and team leaders build consensus among members of a group. *Consensus* is a state of mutual agreement among members of a group where all legitimate concerns of individuals have been addressed to the satisfaction of the group.

Rules for Reaching Consensus is designed as a "how-to" book with a specific step-by-step process for reaching consensus in group meetings or teams. While the language speaks to businesspeople, the process is applicable to private, public, and nonprofit organizations.

Chapter 1, "Collective Decision Making," provides a perspective on traditional group decision making using democratic, majority rule. An alternative approach, consensus decision making, is proposed. Benefits and common misconceptions about the consensus process are addressed.

Chapter 2, "Overview of the Consensus Meeting," provides a big-picture look at consensus-management meetings. It explains how to conduct the beginning, middle, and end of meetings, as well as how to define meeting roles and set an effective agenda.

Chapter 3, "Preconsensus Process," discusses who the group is, what consensus is, and how the group will reach consensus.

Chapter 4, "The Consensus Process and Rules," is the "how-to" section and includes a step-by-step process and rules for reaching consensus in meetings. The three stages of the consensus process are outlined. Stage 1 covers the presentation and clarification of proposals submitted for consensus decision. Stage 2 relates to resolving concerns. Stage 3 examines further closing options.

Chapter 5, "Tips for Facilitators," provides a number of techniques for facilitating the consensus process.

Chapter 6, "Consensus Management," examines the changing roles of management and managers in the twenty-first century. Ideas to foster the spirit and intent of consensus are included.

Consensus Process

Preconsensus

Determine Group Membership
Understand the Meaning of Consensus
Agree on Group Purpose, Values,
    and Authority
Set Standards for Interpersonal Behavior

Stage 1: Understand the Proposal

1.1   State the Proposal
1.2   Clarify the Proposal
1.3   State Concerns
1.4   1st Call for Consensus

Stage 2: Resolve Concerns

2.1   List All Concerns
2.2   Resolve Concerns
2.3   2nd Call for Consensus
2.4   Evaluate Group Purpose and Values
2.5   3rd Call for Consensus
2.6   Evaluate Individual Motives
2.7   Final Call for Consensus

Stage 3: Closing Options

3.1   Contract for More Time
3.2   Presenter Withdraws Proposal
3.3   Concerned Members Withdraw or
      Stand Aside
3.4   Conduct Straw Poll
3.5   Send Proposal to a Subgroup
3.6   Create Community Building
3.7   Conduct Supermajority Vote
3.8   Exclude Members

Collective Decision Making

We are proud of our democratic heritage where governance is vested in the people instead of a single ruler or class. When collective decisions are warranted or required, we are conditioned to vote using the majority rule. The majority rule means that as few as 51 percent of the members of a group can make the decision.

Traditionally, collective decision making by majority rule has been the domain of community groups, legislative bodies, and other public forum groups. At first glance the idea of collective decision making in private or public organizations appears unreasonable and unworkable. The notion that a group of people can make a quicker or better decision through consensus than a sole decision maker seems to run counter to a hierarchical structure.

However, downsizing, decentralization, and creation of teams are breaking down the traditional hierarchal, command and control, superior-subordinate style of management. Authority is shifting from those in positions of power to those who can apply their knowledge to solve a problem. The role of the manager is shifting from being the sole decision maker to being a builder of teams who makes decisions.

The ideas of teams, team building, and facilitating teams is still relatively new. The greatest problem faced by teams and the team builder is who makes the decision. Does the group act in a consultative capacity to the manager, or is it in a decision-making capacity? If it is in a decision-making capacity, what form of collective decision making does the group use—majority rule or consensus?

Changing times force us to look at the benefits and misconceptions of consensus decision making.

Benefits of Consensus

In today's business environment, where outside competition is so great, organizational survival depends on internal cooperaion. Most organizations are plagued by internal competition for resources and for personal advancement. Some managers believe that internal competition is a motivating force. Yet, internal competition manifests itself in power struggles, battles between divisions and departments, backbiting, and poor interpersonal human relationships.

Internal competition diffuses corporate energy, misdirects resources, increases costs, and lowers morale. It generally reduces productivity at everyone's expense—owners, managers, and workers. It also reduces the competitive advantage of the organization.

Many organizational leaders believe that workers don't care about the needs and goals of the organization. Many workers believe that their organization is dehumanizing and does not care about them. We-they attitudes and "what's-in-it-for-me" thinking are outdated modes of behavior.

In seeking mutual agreement, the consensus process fosters individual differences, personal self-reliance and self-esteem, creativity and innovation, cooperative attitudes, improved interpersonal communications and relationships, responsibility, and accountability.

As managers and teams follow the process in both its letter and spirit, the organization will change from a counterproductive, internally competitive organization to an internally cooperative, synergistic enterprise. The real competitive advantage of an organization lies in the synergy of its collective work force.

Misconceptions About Consensus

Some managers are reluctant to use consensus decision making because they believe that it takes too much time and that collective decisions are not as good as individual decisions.

Consensus decision making may take more time, since more people will have to mutually agree on a proposal, but the idea that it takes *too* much time is erroneous. The time it takes a single decision maker to deliberate depends upon his or her personality, experience, and training. Some individuals are more decisive than others. Easy decisions take less time than difficult ones. This is also true of collective decision making, which depends upon the collective makeup, experience, and training of the group in the consensus process.

There is a common misconception that consensus management means that all decisions, no matter how insignificant, must be made by consensus. This is not true. Groups can empower individuals, small representative teams, or large bodies to make decisions.

Everybody in the organization does not have to agree before a decision can be made. Consensus does not means unanimity or 100 percent agreement on everything by everybody. Consensus is not conformity.

Rather, consensus is the mutual feeling that all concerns have been addressed. What is required is that everyone has been heard and understood. Time lost in collective decision making is regained at the implementation stage. The net increase in productivity is significant and synergistic.

Misconceptions about the quality of collective decisions versus the quality of top-down decisions stem, in part, from traditional beliefs about the roles of managers and workers. Some managers still perceive workers as ignorant, uneducated, adversarial laborers. The Industrial Age's superior-subordinate organizational structure carried an underlying assumption that managers were better than their subordinates.

While these structures and points of view may have made sense in the nineteenth century, they are no longer valid. Knowledge workers today have a greater intellectual, financial, and emotional investment in the needs, purposes, and profits of the organization. Knowledge workers are better educated and more self-reliant than workers in the past.

Research indicates that collective decision making actually produces higher quality decisions than those from single decision makers. Collective minds can generate more diverse and creative perspectives. Those who are closest to and responsible for the implementation of decisions are also in the best position to know, understand, and anticipate problems that may arise at the implementation stage.

Many managers sacrifice quality decisions for expediency. There is often an underlying assumption that speedy decisions are more important than good decisions. Too frequently, half-hearted executive decisions are implemented, only to drag on at great cost to organizational cash flow and morale. The best decisions are synergistic and are implemented efficiently and effectively.

Management resistance toward consensus is largely based on anxiety about change and the unknown. Few managers are knowledgeable or experienced in consensus decision making or the consensus process. The whole idea often is alien to what they have been taught about management and decision making.

This book will help managers understand the concept of consensus, see the value of the process, and learn how to use it. We encourage you to get experience using the consensus process because we believe your future depends upon being able to facilitate interpersonal relationships and collective decision making within teams.

Overview of the Consensus Meeting

There are many good books on running meetings and it is not our intent to repeat the ideas and techniques presented in those books. We *do* want to call attention to meeting dynamics that support the consensus process.

Meeting Setup

A circle is the best seating configuration for creating consensus. Ninety percent of communication is nonverbal, so team members must be able to see each other.

Ideally, there should be no barriers, such as tables or other people, between any members. A round or oval table is preferable to a long, rectangular table. The idea is to find the best way to accommodate everyone in a face-to-face seating arrangement.

Flip chart paper can be taped to the walls to record group ideas, thoughts, or processes. This helps provide common understanding and group cohesion.

Beginning the Meeting

Introductions

Meetings should begin with a review of the group's purpose and an introduction of everybody present. New members need to be introduced to old members and vice versa. This facilitates a more open environment.

When introducing new members to the group, explain the reason for their participation, give a synopsis of their background and achievements, and identify the strengths that they contribute toward the group's purpose or mission. Welcome new members warmly and integrate them into the group as quickly as possible.

Effective consensus leaders can use introductions to create positive feelings and group unity by mentioning the individual strengths of both the old and new members.

Moment of Silence

It is quite common for groups to kick off meetings by collectively focusing their minds on the matters at hand. A variety of customs or rituals are used, such as flag salutes, invocations, or group songs or slogans.

One form of focusing is a moment of silence. The group leader calls for a minute of silence so that members can focus on the purpose of the group and the spirit of working creatively to reach mutual agreement.

Roles and Their Functions

Typically people need to serve in at least four roles for a consensus meeting: facilitator, minutes-taker, timekeeper, and monitor.

Facilitator. The facilitator is not a director or a boss. In contrast to the traditional role of director, boss, or group chair, the facilitator plays the role of observer. The group sets the agenda and turns it over to the facilitator for execution. The facilitator's job is to hold the group to the contract it made when it set the agenda and assigned times to the items.

If a facilitator happens to be a manager or supervisor, he or she must be able to transcend any traditional role and mind-set. Otherwise, he or she should turn the role over to another group member.

Minutes-Taker. The minutes-taker is crucial in recording the exact wording of proposals and of any modifications that come up. The facilitator relies on the minutes-taker to remind the group precisely what it has agreed to. It is easy for group members to leave meetings with very different ideas about the decisions that were made.

Timekeeper. The timekeeper works with the facilitator to hold the group to the times allotted for agenda items and to pace the group through that time. Periodically, the timekeeper will remind the group of the time left for an agenda item and will announce when the time is up.

Monitor. The monitor observes the emotional flow of the meeting. While the facilitator focuses on the overt content and agreed-upon process of the meeting, the monitor focuses on the people and their interaction. He or she (or a pair, if possible) may need to intervene when tempers flare, to remind the group of its common purpose and values, and to call for breaks or time-outs. Monitors may also admonish the members to be sensitive to the need of the less vocal members to speak and to contribute ideas.

Scribe. A scribe is useful when the group moves into the resolution of concerns. The scribe records comments on flip charts, chalkboard, or marking board for all to see.

There are many combinations of roles, and your group will decide which are appropriate as time goes on.

Encourage the rotation of roles and functions among the membership in the interest of training everyone to perform the various tasks. If the group is large enough, roles can be shared by teams of two or more. Co-facilitators can divide up the agenda and alternate. With co-facilitators, one facilitator can take more of a contract-keeping role while the other assists in monitoring. Sometimes a facilitator will want a break from acting as a disinterested spectator and may wish to address an agenda item. With co-facilitators, this is possible. Facilitation team pairings can be routinely shifted to keep the group fresh.

Setting the Agenda

The agenda should be developed in advance by group members and reviewed at the beginning of the meeting for any additions or deletions. There are typically three categories of topics for discussion: reports (recent events or committee work), proposals (for group decision), and open discussion (problem solving and brainstorming). The agenda should also include announcements (short items not reflecting any group process), the setting of subsequent meeting dates and agendas, and an evaluation of the meeting process.

The group creates consensus on its priorities by allocating time to each agenda item. Members should be realistic in assessing the amount of time an item will take. Frequently the time necessary for discussion is underestimated. Prioritizing through time allocations helps to ensure that important business gets handled and not just whatever happened to be first on the list.

As the group works together, members will develop an increasingly accurate sense of time. The agenda becomes a group contract that the facilitator oversees. If time on an item is running out, the facilitator asks the group to come to closure or to change the contract, either extending the length of the meeting or subtracting time from another item. Group spirit is always buoyed by meetings that run on time.

Whatever form the agenda takes, it is important to remember that consensus is only used for making decisions. Summaries of committee action or a call for volunteers to help implement a decision previously made do not require consensus.

Trust is a critical factor in consensus. Consensus can only be reached when each member comes to the process confident that the other members are speaking in good faith. Trust can rarely be built in a meeting with a tight agenda filled with business items. It is most effectively created in settings where people are free to speak their feelings without fear of ostracism or reprisal.

We will deal with techniques for fostering community in Chapter 4, Stage 3, "Closing Options." For now, consider what you can do in your meeting cycle to encourage trust, respect, integrity, and community. Perhaps the group needs to schedule occasional social gatherings to deal with the personal side of business.

Conducting the Meeting

When the time comes for a group or team to make a decision, it is time for a specific sequence of steps that will create consensus. We delineate these steps in Chapter 4. For now, remember that consensus is a process of decision making in which all legitimate concerns of group members are addressed to the satisfaction of the group. Ideas for action must be brought to the group in the form of a proposal.

The Proposal

A proposal is a positive statement of a possible action for the group to take. It must be clear to the group what decision it is being asked to make. In our model of consensus, we will go through three levels of process: understanding the proposal, resolving concerns, and closing options. The proposal can regard the establishment of a policy, a particular plan to implement existing policy, or anything requiring group commitment or action.

Brainstorming, while extremely valuable, is not a proposal. A necessary report on an event or a committee's progress is not a proposal. Often meetings will not require any consensus process because the group will not be asked to make decisions.

Some proposals may come from outside sources, such as other teams, groups, or higher levels of a hierarchy. Some proposals will be generated by members of the group. The group must decide who may introduce proposals to the group. Should any individual be free to propose, or should proposals undergo group process prior to arrival on a meeting agenda?

If the group is large enough or has enough time, we recommend that subgroups bring proposals to the full group. Often an idea can be sufficiently refined in advance by a small group to gain easy consensus at a meeting. A small group also might see concerns or objections to which a single presenter may be blind.

It is a good idea to float ideas to other members of the group before forming a proposal, especially to members who might have a particular interest in the decision. In order to effectively communicate the decision the group is being asked to make, the facilitator should review the proposal before the meeting starts.

Ending the Meeting

A Summary of Tasks Taken

The minutes-taker should remind the group's members of their decisions. They should also be reminded of any commitments made by individuals or subgroups.

Evaluation

All meetings should end with an evaluation of the meeting itself. Evaluation should focus strictly on how the meeting was run and should not revisit the agenda items. Evaluation includes the positive aspects of the meeting as well as how subsequent meetings can be improved. This is a good time for gauging each individual's feelings about his or her opportunity to participate and be heard.

Adjournment

Before adjourning, set the time and place for the next meeting. People should be encouraged to bring their appointment books. It is easier to coordinate future meetings with everyone in one place. Also review any items the group wants included on the agenda for subsequent meetings.

Consensus
Meeting Procedures

1. Arrange seating to facilitate face-to-face interaction

2. Review group's purpose

3. Introduce all people

4. Use a moment of silence to focus on group's purpose

5. Select members for necessary roles and functions

6. Set agenda topics, priorities, and time limits

7. Conduct meeting

8. Evaluate meeting's purpose, values, commitments, and procedures

9. Set time, place, and agenda for next meeting

10. Adjourn

3

Preconsensus Process

Determine Group Membership
Understand the Meaning of Consensus
Agree on Group Purpose, Values,
    and Authority
Set Standards for Interpersonal Behavior

Before any group can effectively use consensus decision making, several things will have to be clearly defined: who the group is, what consensus is, and how the group will reach consensus. This is what we call the Preconsensus Process.

The Preconsensus Process focuses on the following four areas of agreement:

1. Determine group membership

2. Understanding the meaning of consensus

3. Agree on group purpose, values, and authority

4. Set strandards for interpersonal behavior

Determine Group Membership

Who is in the group? Which people will be involved in the decision-making process?

Sometimes the group is defined by someone else. Sometimes it is self-constructed by volunteers. In any case, it is important to define the group and to recognize the decision makers.

One way of defining membership is to examine the impact of the decisions to be made by the group. Who will be directly impacted by the decision? Who will be indirectly impacted? Who will be responsible for the decision's implementation? Whose support is needed?

The group should include members representing those affected by the decision, those implementing the decision, and those supporting the implementation. This is an excellent formula for the speedy, efficient implementation of decisions.

Another aspect of determining membership is commitment. Is it wise to allow people with no commitment to the group to have decision-making power? Think about the commitments and responsibilities that go with group membership. Will there be obligations to at-tend a certain number of meetings? Will new members have any formal training in the group's process? Will some group members be decision makers and others observers only?

Without an agreed-upon set of responsibilities for members, consensus breaks down.

Understand the Meaning of Consensus

Consensus is a state of collective agreement. It may be defined as follows:

> *A state of mutual agreement among members of a group where all legitimate concerns of individuals have been addressed to the satisfaction of the group.*

Mutual Agreement

There is group solidarity in sentiment and belief.

Agreement does not mean conformity, where all group members think alike. Nor does it mean that just a majority of the members agree or that everyone in the group agrees about everything.

Mutual agreement does mean that members share the sentiment or belief that all legitimate concerns have been addressed. It is felt more than it is measured. It manifests itself in cooperation as opposed to the competition exhibited in decision making by majority rule. Consensus has more to do with intent and spirit than it does with the letter of the process.

All Legitimate Concerns Are Addressed

These are points of view that relate to the assumptions, implications, and outcomes of a proposal that might adversely affect the organization or be in conflict with its purpose and values. The group itself must discern the differences between the group's stated purpose and values and any individual's agenda.

Each individual has the opportunity to express his or her concerns, and those concerns have been heard, understood, and considered by the members before arriving at a consensus decision.

Consensus deals with human judgment—the heart as well as the mind. Appreciating and becoming skillful at reading these subtleties is important to the understanding of consensus and the process for reaching it.

Agree on Group Purpose, Values, and Authority

Members need to mutually agree on the purpose, values, and authority of the group. They need to know what tasks they have to accomplish and with what authority. It is easy to assume that every group member has the same notion of the group's common purpose, vision, or task. If you want to see just how divergent people's notions are, try drafting a short statement of group purpose.

A group mission statement documents what the group is setting out to do. This positive statement of purpose also implies what the group is *not* setting out to do.

Is your task to develop a plan, program, or proposal, or are you deliberating on someone else's? Will your decisions be final and binding for implementation, or will you only make recommendations to a higher authority? Do you have authority to commit funds and, if so, how much?

Group members need to know the composition of the group and what expertise or perspective each member might contribute in the decision-making process. They also need to know whether the group is an ad hoc or ongoing group. Consensus is more easily reached when the decision-making body understands its relationship to the larger body of which it is a part. What is your relationship, if any, to other decision-making bodies?

Members need to have an understanding of the goals, purpose, and values of the larger organization to which they belong if they are to address legitimate concerns. Aside from the obvious purpose of making a profit, every organization has its own distinct mission and set of values. Organizations today are becoming more customer-centered, recognizing both internal and external customers. Quality, communication, teamwork, cooperative action, self-management, responsibility, and accountability are emphasized.

The process of drafting even the most obvious statement of purpose will go a long way toward getting the group on the same wavelength. At the beginning of *each* meeting the group needs to be reminded of its purpose. All decision making must adhere to this stated purpose.

Set Standards for Interpersonal Behavior

The group must agree on certain standards of behavior. Good interpersonal relationships among group members are essential to reaching consensus. Listening with the intent of understanding another person's perspective is the key to collective decision making. The group must agree that diverse perspectives are valuable, not detrimental, in making the best decision. Group leaders foster the consensus process by valuing and encouraging individual differences. Reminding members of this rule before and during meetings can reduce or avoid judgments, competition, and arguments.

It is imperative that individual members agree that their purpose is to come to consensus on the *best* decision after they have understood as many different perspectives as time permits. They are working cooperatively to make the best decision in support of the purposes, goals, values, and mission of the organization.

The Consensus Process and Rules

The consensus process is divided into three stages.

- *Stage 1:* Submitted proposals are reviewed for understanding and concerns.

- *Stage 2:* The group attempts to resolve concerns.

- *Stage 3:* Closing options are examined.

Stage 1: Understand the Proposal

> 1.1 State the Proposal
> 1.2 Clarify the Proposal
> 1.3 State Concerns
> 1.4 1st Call for Consensus

State the Proposal

The proposal is presented to each member in written form by a single presenter, acting as an individual or on behalf of an internal subgroup or an outside source. If possible, the presenter will distribute the draft of the proposal prior to the meeting.

1.2 Clarify the Proposal

The facilitator opens the floor for clarifying questions. The purpose is to ensure that group members have a clear and common understanding of what is being proposed. This is a time to clarify the proposal, *not* to raise objections or concerns about its merits, impact, or effects. It is appropriate for members to suggest ways of improving the proposal as accepted. Any suggested modifications should be recorded by the minutes-taker.

1.3 State Concerns

Once the group is satisfied that the proposal is clearly understood, the facilitator asks if anyone has any concerns with the proposal as stated. What is being sought are all *legitimate concerns*. As pointed out earlier, legitimate concerns are possible consequences of the proposal that might adversely affect the organization or common good or that are in conflict with the purpose and values of the group.

The group facilitator should remind the group of the definition of legitimate concerns as concerns are presented.

It is imperative to allow ample time to receive responses from shy or less articulate people. One obstacle to overcome in reaching group consensus is to ensure that quiet, shy, and less articulate individuals do not feel that their ideas, opinions, or perspectives are discounted because others are more aggressive or outspoken. The facilitator must create an environment in which people are encouraged to share their opinions and perspectives.

1.4 1st Call for Consensus

If no concerns are raised, the facilitator may declare that the group has reached consensus, or he or she may ask the group, "Have we reached a consensus?" If there are no objections, the group has reached consensus.

Stage 2: Resolve Concerns

 List All Concerns

If concerns are stated, the facilitator and the scribe should try to distill each one into a short phrase. A co-facilitator or the scribe should write these summations in full view of the group. Group members should assist in summarizing stated concerns.

Writing concerns on a chalkboard or flip chart page helps the group to focus on the concern, not the presenter or the person stating the concern. The facilitator can use this process to build group cohesion, consensus, and team spirit by reminding the group of the distinction between legitimate and personal concerns. Depending upon the sophistication of the group, the facilitator might even ask the group to validate each concern as it is presented by asking the question: "Might this be a *legitimate* concern?" Again it is imperative that ample time be allowed in order to ensure participation by shy or less articulate people.

Avoid Repeating Concerns

Members may want to clarify concerns, but should refrain from repeating concerns already listed on the board. There is a tendency (a hold-over from our voting processes) to repeat or second a concern in order to give it more weight with the group. There is also a tendency (a hold-over of our advocacy or competitive processes) to lobby a concern by repeating it or rephrasing it in several different ways. No concern needs to be repeated or seconded.

Once all the concerns are listed, it is useful to spend time having the group look over all of the concerns as a whole. They can then check for duplication, clarity, and wording to ensure that they have a list of unique concerns.

After the group has finished listing its concerns, the facilitator can judge how close to consensus the proposal is. If the concerns are many and the time short, the proposal may be continued to a later meeting.

If time permits, the group members must now put their heads together and attempt to integrate the concerns into the proposal. Rather than thinking competitively to either pass or reject the idea, the group seeks consensus by thinking cooperatively.

2.2 Resolve Concerns

The proposal is explained or changed to address concerns. The presenter has first option to resolve the listed concerns by using one of the following techniques:

1. Clarify the proposal

2. Change the proposal

3. Explain why the proposal as stated is not in conflict with the group's values

4. See if those with concerns will stand aside.

Stand Aside

Group members stand aside when they have concerns about a proposal, but they can live with it. Standing aside signals that the person feels his or her concern has been heard, understood, and considered, although not necessarily accepted, by the group in its final decision.

Stand-asides differ from parliamentary abstentions. People may abstain for numerous reasons (i.e., ignorance, ambivalence, or political posture), but standing aside is an option only for people with concerns. Standing aside does not remove the concern from the list. If decisions are made that include the stand asides, the appropriate concerns should be noted by the minutes-taker.

Cross Through Concerns

If those stating concerns are satisfied with the presenter's explanation of or changes to the proposal, they indicate so by having the listing on the board erased or crossed through. Other group members may assist the presenter in resolving concerns.

While some claim consensus cannot work in large groups, others argue that consensus becomes more likely the larger the group gets: the more minds, the better the odds someone will come up with a perfect solution.

Resolving concerns is a creative process with a goal to produce the best possible decision. Often a best decision is finding a *third* way; something in between the typical either/ or, right/wrong, or black/white mind-set.

2.3 **2nd Call for Consensus**

If all the concerns listed have been resolved, the facilitator asks if there are any unresolved concerns. If there are none, the facilitator announces the group has reached consensus.

2.4 Evaluate Group Purpose and Values

If listed concerns have been adequately discussed and remain unresolved, and concerned members are unwilling to stand aside, the facilitator moves the group to a new level of resolution in which it examines the nature of the concerns. At this level, the discussion moves beyond the impersonal evaluation of the proposal and of listed concerns to probe group purpose and values.

The group needs to assess how the unresolved concerns relate to the group's purpose and to the larger audience that its decision represents. If the group is strongly divided over a proposal, perhaps there is ambiguity around one of the elements agreed upon during the Preconsensus Process. These agreements need to be revisited with each concern. Is there disagreement about the group's purpose or mission statement? Is there disagreement about the group's shared values? Do two or more of the values conflict?

The group may need to reconsider the basic elements of the Preconsensus Process and then reconstruct the consensus it felt it had in the beginning.

In the case of countervailing values, the group may have to decide which value takes precedence, or what version of the proposal gives both values equal influence.

2.5 3rd Call for Consensus

Once the unresolved concerns are scrutinized in light of the group's purpose and values, the facilitator will identify one of the following conclusions:

1. The member is not willing to withdraw the concern or stand aside.

2. The concerned member withdraws the concern or stands aside.

3. The member withdraws the concern based on the group purpose evaluation.

In the first case, the remaining concern is noted by the minutes-taker. In the second case, the facilitator announces that the group has reached consensus, and the minutes-taker notes the concern in the minutes. In the third case, the facilitator announces that the group has reached consensus. However, having reached the first conclusion, the facilitator may note that the group is still at an impasse. It is time for the next level of evaluation.

2.6 Evaluate Individual Motives

If there has been thorough discussion of group purpose and values and how they relate to the unresolved concerns, and individuals have been heard, understood, and considered in the total decision, any further impasse is most likely due to personal dynamics or vested interests, not group purpose. Concerns based on ego or vested interests originate with the question: "What is best for me and mine?" rather than "What is best for the group?" While vested concerns are often phrased in terms of strategy or issues, there are underlying tensions about authority, rights, personality conflicts, competition, or lack of trust.

Most likely, these kinds of concerns won't be resolved in a business meeting or work session. If team members aren't trusting each other to speak and act in good faith for the good of the group, it is impossible to proceed. Trust is a prerequisite to the consensus process.

2.7 Final Call for Consensus

If a member with an unresolved concern admits to an inappropriate motive, the unresolved concern is considered resolved. The facilitator announces that the group has reached consensus.

If any concerns remain, the facilitator moves to Stage 3, "Closing Options."

Stage 3: Closing Options

> 3.1 Contract for More Time
> 3.2 Presenter Withdraws Proposal
> 3.3 Concerned Members Withdraw or Stand Aside
> 3.4 Conduct Straw Poll
> 3.5 Send Proposal to a Subgroup
> 3.6 Create Community Building
> 3.7 Conduct Supermajority Vote
> 3.8 Exclude Members

We have outlined a very thorough process for reaching consensus. Groups need to give themselves the time necessary to go through this penetrating and painstaking process.

Some groups will reach consensus without moving very far up the ladder of resolution. Groups with solid agreements, good subgroup work on proposals, and ego detachment will breeze through faster than you can say, "The ayes have it!"

If time runs out for group deliberation, the agenda item must be closed. When the time-keeper indicates it is time to close, the facilitator gives the presenter the courtesy of choosing closing options. The more options facilitators and presenters have, the quicker the group can create consensus.

3.1 Contract for More Time

When the group sets the initial agenda and allocates time blocks, it makes a contract with itself to be enforced by the facilitator. If the presenter wants to extend time on an issue, he or she must renegotiate the contract.

Additional time must be subtracted from other items or added to the total meeting length. Since the group has already spent time working out the initial contract, the additional time option should only be allowed if there is unanimity. A single objection torpedoes the request for more time.

3.2 Presenter Withdraws Proposal

A presenter may, with the consent of any sub-group member, withdraw the proposal from further consideration and allow the group to proceed.

3.3 Concerned Members Withdraw or Stand Aside

Those with unresolved concerns may opt to withdraw their concerns voluntarily or stand aside, allowing the proposal to pass.

3.4 Conduct Straw Poll

A nonbinding show of hands might be useful in gaining a sense of the group. The results of a straw poll might sway members' opinions about the proposal or the unresolved concerns. If very few members favor the proposal, the presenter might find it easier to withdraw it. If very few share the unresolved concerns, the concerned members might find it easier to stand aside. An evenly divided straw poll indicates further work is needed.

3.5 Send Proposal to a Subgroup

Depending upon the size and structure of the group, the facilitator or other group member may suggest that the proposal undergo modifications in a small group outside the main meeting.

Subgroup to Return Proposal

This small group could be an existing subgroup or an ad hoc committee established for the purpose of working on the proposal. The larger group may ask the small group to bring the proposal back in a form that addresses the concerns as outlined.

Empowered Subgroup

In some cases, where time is of the essence or the matter is procedural rather than substantive, a small group may be empowered to come to consensus and to proceed, in the name of the full group, without further permission. Whatever form it takes, a subgroup should include everyone with interest in or concerns about the proposal.

3.6 Create Community Building

If the proposal has brought to light underlying problems with group dynamics or personality clashes, the facilitator may suggest a session strictly for community building. Such sessions could involve formal mediation from third parties outside the conflict. They might be informal social gatherings, structured team building groups, or other processes for developing interpersonal dynamics.

3.7 Conduct Supermajority Vote

It is possible to structure a vote to close the decision. It has been argued that a simple majority vote is more democratic than a hung jury consensus. In trying to avoid the "Tyranny of the Majority," we do not embrace the "Tyranny of the Minority." A vote requiring a 66 to 90 percent majority for passage could approximate consensus if the group has exhausted its ability to cooperate.

3.8 Exclude Members

If members realize they are at dramatic odds with the group, they may want to exclude themselves and allow the group to proceed. The group, out of legitimate concern for its own health, may choose to exclude members it feels are destructive. It is important to remember that the group has the final responsibility for determining which concerns are germane to the decision at hand. Individuals have the responsibility of making a good case for each concern, but the time comes when the group must come first.

Consensus Process Flow Chart

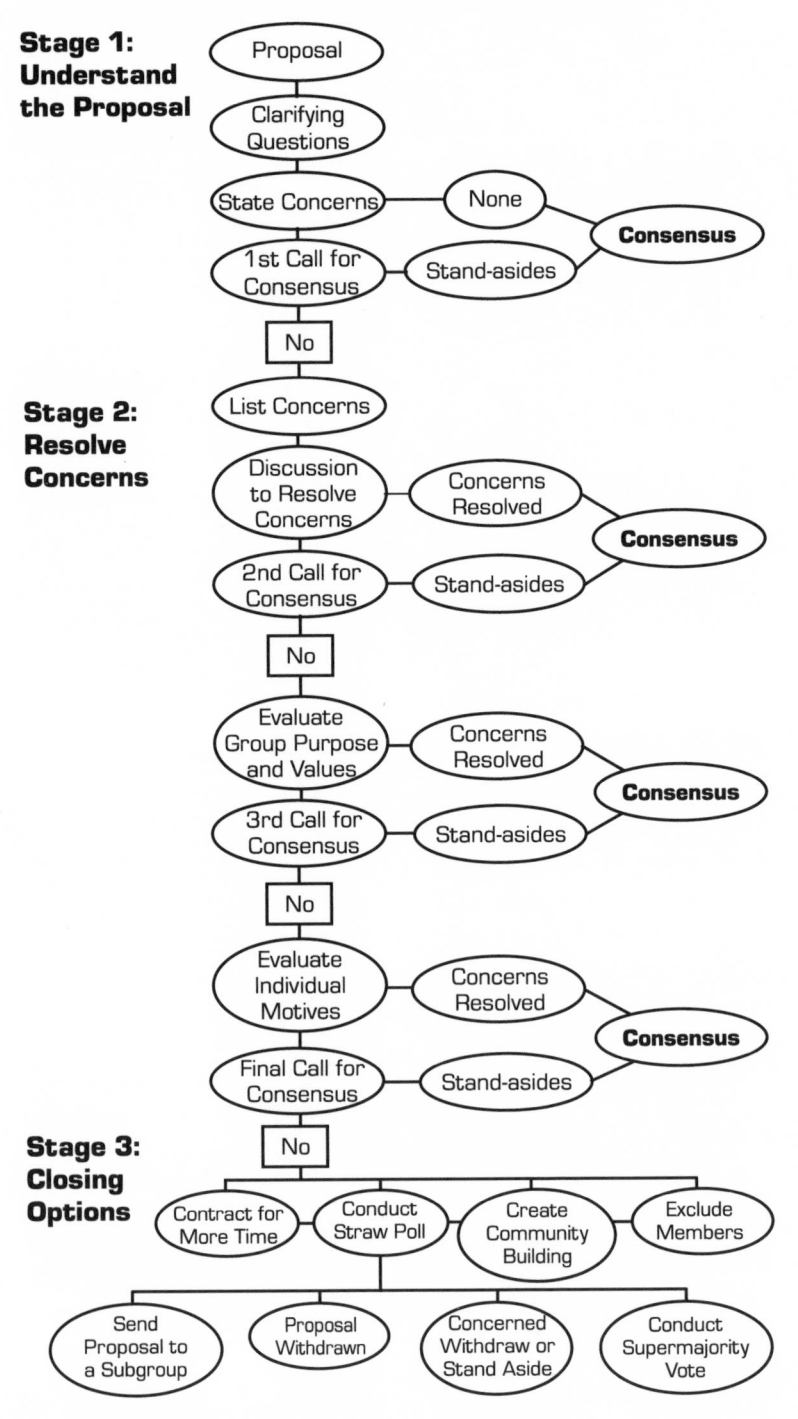

Stage 1: Understand the Proposal

Proposal

Clarifying Questions

State Concerns — None

1st Call for Consensus — Stand-asides — **Consensus**

No

Stage 2: Resolve Concerns

List Concerns

Discussion to Resolve Concerns — Concerns Resolved

2nd Call for Consensus — Stand-asides — **Consensus**

No

Evaluate Group Purpose and Values — Concerns Resolved

3rd Call for Consensus — Stand-asides — **Consensus**

No

Evaluate Individual Motives — Concerns Resolved

Final Call for Consensus — Stand-asides — **Consensus**

Stage 3: Closing Options

No

Contract for More Time | Conduct Straw Poll | Create Community Building | Exclude Members

Send Proposal to a Subgroup | Proposal Withdrawn | Concerned Withdraw or Stand Aside | Conduct Supermajority Vote

5

Tips for Facilitators

The word "facilitator" has been carefully chosen. Drawn from Latin roots, it means "one who makes things easy." In a consensus-based group, every member has a responsibility to facilitate the group. In contrast to groups with chairs, vice-chairs, and other hierarchical structures, a consensus group is a group of leaders.

One or two people are chosen each meeting to perform the formal function of facilitator. The facilitator's primary job is to hold the group to its various agreements, which include meeting protocols, the agenda, and time allocations. These agreements were not created single-handedly, and the group should appreciate the facilitator's role as enforcer.

Remember, reaching consensus is simply a process of discerning the sense of the group. The purpose in holding the group accountable to its agreements is to help it discern its own sense. A facilitator must suspend his or her vested interest in the decision's outcome and work to sense the group's will.

In general, a facilitator is the tour guide through the group process—summarizing its progress, reminding members where they are in the process, and suggesting what steps are next.

Understanding the Proposal

The group needs to arrive at a common understanding of what decision it is being asked to make. The following techniques can help.

Premeeting Proposal Circulation

The more a proposal can be circulated in advance of a decision-making meeting, the more likely it will be presented in a form acceptable to the group. If you know a proposal is coming up for decision, you can make sure all interested parties (especially those who might have concerns) see the proposal in advance and give input to the presenter or subgroup. A little time spent including people before the meeting goes a long way toward making a meeting run smoothly.

All-Sides Presentation

When presenters outline proposals, they should include a description of how the proposal was conceived and drafted. This description should mention how various concerns were taken into consideration. If a subgroup drafted the proposal, the presentation should include how the subgroup came to consensus. The larger group should know if the smaller group was unified in its process or if there was a lot of dissent. This will help other group members see how the proposal as stated has tried to address their concerns.

Restate the Proposal

Help the group stay on track by restating the proposal at significant junctures. Sometimes group members forget what decision they are being asked to make. As clarifying questions are posed, make sure the presenter has answered them to the group's satisfaction.

Postpone Concerns

Once a proposal has been presented, it is easy for group members to begin raising concerns. Members must respectfully postpone discussion of concerns until the proposal has been fully clarified. Beware of people stating concerns in the form of a question. Ask them to hold on to their concerns until the proposal is fully understood and clarified.

Resolving Concerns

The process of resolving concerns can be a confused melee of voices stating concerns, addressing concerns, suggesting process, or offering points of information in no particular logical progression. The facilitator's job is to distill the legitimate concerns and allow the presenter and other members adequate chance to explain or modify the proposal.

Remain Neutral

A facilitator must remain neutral. All words and actions must promote group process, not a point of view on the decision. If the facilitator has a personal contribution to make on the fate of the proposal, it is best to step out of role for the agenda item in question and to hand facilitation to another member or to an assigned co-facilitator.

Summarize Concerns for Listing

As people state concerns, the facilitator can help summarize and list them on the chalkboard or flip chart paper. This requires some give-and-take with group members in order to accurately phrase the concern to their satisfaction. Often people will basically repeat a concern already listed with a slight nuance that they can call their own. If each phrase does not summarize a distinct concern, the group will wind up with a list of aliases for what amounts to one or two real concerns.

Group Listed Concerns for Summary

A further distillation of concerns can be achieved by grouping similar phrases and concerns. Concerns that seemed distinct when listed separately might later appear to overlap or blend. Grouping gives members a final grasp of the real concerns to be resolved.

Fishbowl

Large groups often engage in lengthy dialogue over controversial proposals because many people want to express support for the proposal or state concerns. To compress this dialogue, the facilitator can arrange a fishbowl exercise in which two or three sides of an issue are personified by two or three speakers. These speakers conduct a two- or three-way dialogue in the center of the circle, allowing the larger group to hear all sides in a relatively speedy fashion.

Relate Concerns to Group Values

We have defined concerns as statements of how the proposal might conflict with the group's purpose or shared values. People often state concerns about a proposal that are more germane to their private sensitivities or sense of strategy than they are to the purpose or values of the group. Whenever possible, an attempt should be made to tie stated concerns to the purpose. Invite members to withdraw extraneous concerns.

Invite Group Members to Stand Aside

Reaching consensus is not necessarily reaching unanimity. Sometimes people don't care for a proposal but can live with the decision the group makes. The group should not be impeded by casual concerns. People are often happy to stand aside on a concern if they feel the group has adequately considered it. In the stating and listing process, the facilitator should feel free to ask a speaker if he or she is willing to stand aside on a concern.

Straw Poll

As previously described, a straw poll is a non-binding show of hands to measure the sense of the group. Because it is unfair to measure the sense of the group before some minimum standard of adequate discussion has occurred, avoid taking straw polls until concerns have been listed.

To emphasize the cooperative nature of a straw poll, it should be presented in terms of freeing people to proceed with discussion or to withdraw or stand aside on concerns. Do not count hands—this is not a vote.

Go-Round

In a go-round, each member of the group has a moment to speak to the issue. Go-rounds offer the refreshing opportunity to hear from less vocal members of a group. They also act as an expanded straw poll in which each member states a position on the decision backed with reasons. For this reason, go-rounds are often preferred to straw polls if time permits.

Small Group Discussion

If a number of people need to speak to a proposal, time may not permit them to do so individually. The group can break into small groups, even groups of two or three, to allow full discussion. Small groups also allow those people who might be shy in front of the large group to speak. Each small group can attempt to reach consensus and then can appoint a speaker to report on its deliberations.

Limit Discussion

The consensus process attempts to provide adequate discussion opportunities for all members.

Still there are those members who tend to dominate the discussion. Members often repeat concerns or explanations unnecessarily. If necessary, limit discussion to avoid domination and repetition.

If the facilitator cannot speak candidly with the offending members, he or she can try a formal process where members cannot speak again until everyone else has had the opportunity. Comments can also be limited to a certain time, i.e., three minutes per speaker.

Hand Signals for Points of Process and Information

Robert's Rules of Order provides for points of order and information. These points are supposed to be neutral and, while germane to the discussion on the floor, not part of the dialogue. Members of consensus-based groups also need, from time to time, to raise issues about the process itself or to give the group information relevant to the decision at hand. We recommend a simple hand signal to indicate such a point: two hands raised. When recognizing someone with two hands raised, make sure he or she is actually raising a point of process or information, not entering the dialogue.

Closing Options

Discussions for decisions are closed when time has run out and members still have unresolved concerns. We won't reiterate the closing options here, but there are things you can do to make closing run smoothly.

Pace the Group

The facilitator should know how much time is allowed for a decision and pace the group through clarification and resolution of concerns appropriately. Help the group allot realistic times to items so discussions aren't always cut short. If half of the allotted time is up and the group is still clarifying the proposal, the facilitator may have to contract then and there or move to closure early.

Five-Minute Warning

The facilitator needs to work with the time-keeper to make sure time for an item doesn't run out before closure. Have the time-keeper provide a five-minute warning, allowing the opportunity to either contract for more time or move to a closing option.

Summarize the Process

Always summarize for the group where they are in the process and how they have come to this point. Distill the unresolved concerns to their bare essence and remind the group exactly what decision it is being asked to make. Summarize for the group what closing options are available.

Monitoring the Process

The emotional flow of a meeting greatly impacts the rational deliberations. For all we know, having a rational discussion is just a complicated way to align personal feelings. All groups feel stress, and members rarely feel comfortable and work well with everyone. Monitors and facilitators must work together in reducing stress, resolving unspoken conflicts, and minimizing distractions.

Breaks

Every group needs a break. Breaks can be built into the agenda or can be called spontaneously by the facilitator or monitor. The group can use the breaks for people to build individual focus (silence, a stretch) or to change the tenor of the interaction (socializing, back rubs, even singing). Breaks should always be appropriately timed and monitored.

Appeal to Senses

Monitors can appeal to the five senses in various ways to bypass the intellectual and reach the emotional. Fear is often mitigated by input to the senses. Try ringing a small, pleasant bell to signal time for speakers or to indicate a tension surge in the group. Pass an object (rock, pillow) from hand to hand to appeal to touch, or a flower to appeal to both touch and smell.

Humor

Nothing mitigates stress in a group like humor. Humor tends to place hot issues into a cooler, less self-important context. Assign someone the role of "Joke Master," ready to intervene at tense moments. Have a hat or bedpan to fine members for talking too much or repeating concerns. Bring a mysterious brown bag and threaten to give members the unknown contents if they take things too seriously. Few of the group's decisions are matters of life and death, and members should be reminded not to take everything seriously.

6

Consensus Management

You might ask, why bother to use consensus decision making? We suspect that if you are currently a manager, team leader, or team builder, you are already trying to create unity, coordination, cooperation, and synergism in your organization. We suspect that you are already seeking consensus in one form or another.

As the global market becomes more dynamic and competitive, organizations must become more efficient, effective, and productive. To do this, organizations are becoming small, dynamic, flexible systems. Organizations are optimizing their systems and work forces to create a synergistic whole.

The Introduction and Chapter 1 suggest that traditional organizational structures are being replaced by new team-oriented approaches that result in networked or webbed organizational structures. The superior-subordinate relationship of the hierarchical structure assumes that some individuals are superior and others are inferior. Managers are considered to be superior, and tradition dictates that they singlehandedly make decisions because their subordinates cannot. This tradition is based on early Industrial Age thinking in which farmers and emigrants coming to the cities to work were considered ignorant, unskilled, and in need of rote training and direction.

In today's age with its highly educated knowledge workers, advanced communications, and breakdown of the hierarchical structure, the superior-inferior philosophy is invalid. The new team-oriented approach and networked organizational structures are creating new management philosophies and new roles and functions for managers.

The underlying philosophy of the consensus process is to create unity while valuing diversity. Today's organizations are seeking to optimize, unify, and create synergy among their diverse resources; they are attempting to create organizational consensus. The authors see a new twenty-first century management philosophy emerging that we call *consensus management*.

Consensus management assumes that each individual is unique and valuable, and each has something to contribute. Diverse individuals, teams, and departments must work together for the common good of the organization. Valuing each other's differences and fostering unity is the underlying assumption of consensus management and consensus decision making. The emerging role and function of the leader-manager is to create unity yet value differences.

Roles and Functions of the Leader-Manager

The role of the leader-manager is shifting to that of a team builder or team leader as opposed to that of a commander and controller. One of the major tasks of the leader-manager is to train people to accept responsibility for problem solving, decision making, and self-management—both as individuals and collectively as a team.

The effective consensus leader has two major functions: one relating to process and structure, the other relating to the spirit and intent of consensus. The focus of this book has been primarily process and structure, but a major challenge for the group leader is to create an environment that fosters the spirit and intent of consensus.

Here are some things you can do to foster the consensus process.

1. *Create Unity*. Inspire people with a vision of the future. Help them seek a higher purpose in working together. Help people

see their interconnectedness and the need for cooperation to meet the group's higher purpose. Focus on responsibilities rather than rights. Redefine intent when members become polarized on process.

2. *Value Diversity.* Value differences of perspective. See different perspectives as opportunities for learning, creativity, and innovation. Seek clarification and learning. The best decisions come from multiple points of view—value all perspectives. Confront prejudice directly, openly, and immediately.

3. *Involve Everybody.* Be inclusive, not exclusive. Include all people—in some way—who will be affected by the outcome of decisions. Involve all members of the group or team in making the decision.

4. *Promote Imagination, Creativity, Innovation.* Americans are trained and rewarded as problem solvers, but problem solving addresses something that already exists. Creativity and innovation bring something new into existence. Imagination is the mother of creativity and innovation. Reward imagination and foster creativity and innovation.

5. *Look for the Third Way.* Individuals in groups tend to polarize, to assume extreme or opposite perspectives. Don't get hung

up on poles of either/or, we/they, right/ wrong, good/bad, win/lose, or for/against. Suggest finding the third way. The third way takes a different perspective than either pole. Encourage individuals or team members who confront each other from opposite extremes to cooperate and create a third approach that incorporates their diverse perspectives. Refocus on intent of group effort and the common good. This fosters innovation and creates joint ownership and unity.

6. *Use Internal Rewards*. Seek ways to create internal rewards verses external rewards. Internal rewards are those things that are naturally rewarding to human beings: a common purpose, the spirit of working together, opportunities to create and innovate, opportunities to learn and grow personally and professionally, having opinions heard and respected, and pride of workmanship.

7. *Promote Value of Learning*. There is a distinction between learning and training. Training is something someone does to you and is based on a Pavlovian conditioning process. It solicits a mindless response based on the stimulus of an outside operator. Learning is something you do of your own volition. Learning uses one's intrinsic abilities. Learning is the way that human

beings can survive rapid change. Provide learning opportunities. Reward personal and professional growth and self-directed learning.

8. *Encourage Self-reliance.* Encourage individuals to be responsible and accountable. Focus on responsibility rather than rights. Reward proactive behavior. Reinforce self-directed behavior.

9. *Encourage Empathetic Listening.* Consensus depends upon members' feelings. All must feel deeply that their particular thoughts and feelings have been expressed, respected, and considered in the final decision. Encourage quiet or reticent members to participate and to share their thoughts, feelings, and experiences. Those who are quiet need time to respond. They are not practiced and need to be sure people care about what they have to say. If they are asked their opinion or point of view, *wait* for the answer. Listen deeply to other's points of view with respect and without judgment, even if these views differ from your own. Listening with empathy requires patience, trust, openness, and, above all, a desire to understand. The leader sets the example.

We are on the threshold of a new age, a new era, a new civilization. Yet we still live with the vestiges of an older age. Today's leaders are caught between two eras. *Robert's Rules of Order* was written to create processes and procedures for reaching decisions by majority rule. *Rules for Reaching Consensus* is designed to provide the processes and procedures for reaching decisions by consensus.

Index

About the Authors

Steven Saint

Steven Saint is an independent journalist covering national and regional affairs for over thirty-five newspapers and magazines. He has been involved in human relations and prodiversity organizations since high school and is currently on the Human Relations Commission for the city of La Mesa, CA. He cofounded the Consensus Institute in 1990 to promote consensus-based decision making in the Green Party and the progressive movement at large. He is currently on the statewide Mediation Panel for the Green Party of California.

James R. Lawson

James R. Lawson, Ph.D., is Executive Director of HMS Associates, a San Diego-based management consulting firm. He has enjoyed an extensive career in business, government, and education and has held significant managerial positions in sales, administrative operations, human resources, and executive management. Dr. Lawson teaches management and organizational behavior courses at the University of Phoenix and writes extensively about leadership, organization structure, and the new organizational paradigm for the twenty-first century.